T0162854

THE ILLUSION OF A PROJECT

Find and Fix
the Disconnect
to the Strategic Plan

MAVIESE A. FISHER

Order this book online at www.trafford.com
or email orders@trafford.com

Most Trafford titles are also available at major online book retailers.

© Copyright 2012 Maviese A. Fisher.
All rights reserved. No part of this publication may be reproduced, stored in a retrieval
system, or transmitted, in any form or by any means, electronic, mechanical, photocopying,
recording, or otherwise, without the written prior permission of the author.

Printed in the United States of America.

ISBN: 978-1-4669-1485-8 (sc)
ISBN: 978-1-4669-1486-5 (hc)
ISBN: 978-1-4669-1487-2 (e)

Library of Congress Control Number: 2012902470

Trafford rev. 03/28/2012

 www.trafford.com

North America & international
toll-free: 1 888 232 4444 (USA & Canada)
phone: 250 383 6864 ♦ fax: 812 355 4082

TABLE OF CONTENTS

Acknowledgements

My sincere thanks and appreciation goes to all of my family members and special friends that have encouraged me to keep writing. I especially want to give a special thank you to my husband, Johnson for his continued support and encouragement in writing this book.

To all of the companies that have given me real world experience in managing projects and programs over the years, without this I could not have written this book.

To all of my fabulous project team members that have made managing projects a pleasure.

To anyone that aspires to manage projects, I truly hope that there is some wisdom in this book that will be of assistance in your journey.

All my Best.

Maviese

CHAPTER 1

INTRODUCING THE ILLUSION

The first thought that the word illusion brings to mind for many people is one of smoke and mirrors, or the visualization of a magician on stage making objects that seem real appear and disappear. Illusions however do not just happen on stage and have nothing to do with smoke and mirrors of the literal kind.

Given the right set of circumstances, anything can appear and disappear especially in a matrix organization. What is even more pointed is that the vast majority of the company divisions today are structured as a matrix organization at some level; you are most likely working in this type of environment right now. It is hard to escape the touch of the matrix. When it works, it works well, more often than not it does not work, and we will talk about that in the next chapter. The matrix structure is seldom alone; it is usually accompanied with the following traits:

- The renouncement of the existing **Intellectual Capital.**

- Exclusive acceptance of the invisible **Virtual Workforce.**

- Bewilderment at the complexity of the **Global Factors.**

- The trendy phenomenon of the immersion of **Off Shore** operations.

You are reading this book because you are most likely wearing one of three hats C, D or P. "C" CIO, Division, or Program/Project level. That being the case means that at some level you are living in this book. You are responsible for, or are working on a project or worse yet a program that belongs to a portfolio of products and services for a company that flags a strategic plan. Sadly enough this is the case more often than not. The problem is that in the vast majority of cases it is not clear what that strategic plan is or what the project / program links are suppose to be to stay in business.

Too often the strategic plan will start to look like an illusion if the people and projects that are executing on the strategy do not have a clear and concise path that leads from the strategic plan to that project. Somehow, that path became compromised with abstract tasks that show up on slides that require magnification to read. It is a sure bet that you have seen a few of these. Too often that path is disconnected and lost in the list of accompanying traits of the matrix environment.

According to a Balanced Scorecard collaborative group analysis of 354 executives of which 49% of the respondents were from C-level positions and 56% were from companies with revenues greater than $1 billion:[1]

- 95 percent of the average workforce does not understand the company's strategy.

- 90 percent of the companies fail to execute on established strategies.

- 85 percent of executive teams spend 60 minutes or less per month discussing strategy.

- 60 percent of companies do not link their budgets to the strategic plan.

Only 10 percent of the companies today actually achieve measurable results in strategy execution. The other 90 percent of the companies are just talking about it.

Why, when, where and just how did this illusional state happen? We have all asked these same questions, if only for a moment, and now in this book we are going to expose several of the main disconnects from the strategic plan to the projects that should be feeding the strategic plan and propose some connective tools to fix the disconnect.

First, let us examine some of the dynamics that are making significant contributions to the disappearance of the paths from the strategic plan and profitability of companies.

The Illusion of a Project takes you behind the stage to show you where, why and how a project comes into existence, what the building blocks are of the project, at what point and where the project becomes an illusion even though the project by itself is successful.

Once you know the potential points where the connection may be broken, you need to expose some of the enablers of that illusive environment. This is important because once the connection is broken the project becomes an illusion, it no longer supports the strategic plan and profitability of the company. Now is the time to ask if this is the right project for the business, or where the project or the connection to that project's needs should be brought back in line with the strategic plan objectives. Too often no one asks. Everyone is focused on where they come in and no one is watching the big picture. Whose job is that any way? Who or what is the enabler?

The enablers can take the form of an illusion if you are not aware of the various forms. Let us look at a snapshot of the platform on which the illusion happens—the Program Process Flow. Figure 1-1 shows us the Program / Project Life Cycle in various stages. Each stage will be explained in detail in the following chapters when we review the Project Process in stages.

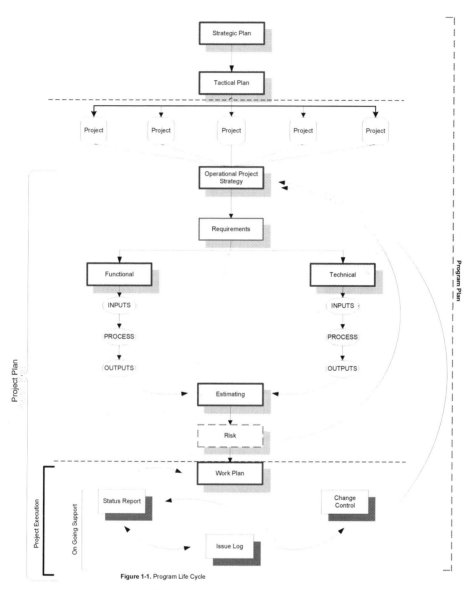

Figure 1-1. Program Life Cycle

(Program Process Flow)

Important to note that the Program Life Cycle starts at the Strategic planning stage and continues through the Ongoing Support stage. Too often, the Program Life Cycle is thought to start at the Operational Project Strategy stage. Enter the first glimpse of the illusive fog that will begin to fade the connection to the strategic plan. Do not let it happen. This is the opportunity to review, yet again, the Strategic Plan of the organization. Make sure that each of the projects are the right project for the organization. Ask the questions! What are the objectives? Why are we doing this? When does this need to be done and can we do it in that period? What are the risks in doing this? Where is this to be performed, where is the support and the execution of the plan coming from? How is this to be performed, by whom? Do not just ask the questions, work the questions, and follow through with action!

Every single project should be able to answer the question of how that project supports the strategic plan. If the decision is to implement an ERP system then the question is how is the ERP system going to support the Strategic Plan. Is the ERP project going to contribute to the profitability or efficiency of the organization? Moreover, if it is then by how much and when? The ERP system should not be implemented until there are answers. Too often new products and services are brought into a company without asking the essential questions, they are viewed as optional questions or disintegrate in the political crossfire, exactly why the connection to the strategic plan never enters into question.

Too little attention is paid to one of the most valuable assets that a company has, that being Intellectual Capital. One reason is that Intellectual Capital is often viewed as an expense not an asset.[2] Only 15% of the value of a company today is attributed to tangible assets; the other 85% of the company's value is attributed to intangible assets. That 85% is the Intellectual Capital that is ignored, overlooked and materializes as one of the spin off divisions housed in one of the off shore locations reachable only as part of the virtual workforce. We address this dilemma later in Chapter 3 and flow into Chapter 4 with the extension of the global factors.

The old saying that "a picture is worth a thousand words" is on point and is exactly what we will paint through Project Parables for a fictitious company called "Illusion Specialist LLP."—a provider of products and services.

Let us get started.

CHAPTER 2

THE MATRIX IS ALIVE—LOOKING THROUGH THE MATRIX

Often when you hear about a matrix managed environment it is accompanied by a list of survival tactics entitled "how to survive . . .". Why do you think that is true? Could it be that the matrix-managed style doesn't fit, not unlike a trendy shoe that everyone is wearing? For some the style is a good compliment for others it simply doesn't fit. The issue is that no one, least of all the shoe sales person, bothers to tell the ill fitted client that the shoe doesn't come in their size. Therefore they find out the hard way and end up with callused and blistered feet. It's not for everyone especially if it is poorly executed. On the other hand, is it that there is nothing wrong with matrix management but rather the execution of matrix management by misinformed or worse yet unknowing management that is wrong?

Matrix management is one of the illusive enablers, and strangely enough, matrix management exists today in the vast majority of organizations in one form or another. It is no longer the buzzword that it was during the 80's, books are no longer being written and very little is said about it yet it is very much alive today. The scary aspect of this is that most management today have no idea that they are managing in the matrix nor can they describe the type of organizational structure that their division or company is modeled after. How then are they managing?

- You can't manage what you can't control.

- You can't control what you can't measure.

- You can't measure what you can't define.

- You can't define what is an unknown illusion.[3]

So let us first talk about the **illusional background**, the formation of matrix management, de-mystify, and de-illusionize it. Follow that by **defining** what matrix management is, finding a **measurement** of what works, and just what **controls** make it work. Then, and only then, can the matrix be managed.

The illusional background

Matrix management is not new; it has been around since the building of pyramids and probably before that. During the mid 1960's the National Aeronautics and Space Administration (NASA) developed the first formal matrix organizational structure. It needed to pull together multiple key functions in a project none of which could be compromised. Traditional project management structures would not allow the type of cohesion that was required, so NASA created that environment known today as the matrix organization.

Matrix management models have originated from three diverse sources—project management, product management and functional authority. The distribution of these sources will be determined by the type of organization that is engaged. Moreover, it is usually uneven.[5]

- Project management is by far the strongest influencer of this type of management. Project management typically pulls from multiple sources to synergistically create a product or service.

- Product management has fueled matrix management through the indirect affiliation with the need to control large programs involving large areas of manufacturing companies.

- Functional authority that is represented on most organizational charts with dotted lines of authority. The dotted lines are the right of passage for the matrix environment.

Figure 2-6 Matrix in Motion

Defining what the matrix is

According to Knight, there are two main classes that matrix organizations fall under—leadership matrix and the co-ordination matrix.[6]

The leadership matrix

(a) presumes that people tend, if left to themselves, to pursue their own ends, which are likely to be related to their professional, specialist goals, and need galvanizing into working on the organization's goals;

(b) needs drive, motivation and leadership towards tackling the task goals;

(c) needs the leaders of the lateral groups to have influence and status, so that they are not dominated by the heads of the vertical groups;

(d) requires the lateral groups to be cohesive and strongly motivated to solve the problems necessary to complete the task.

The co-ordination matrix

(a) presumes that people are rational and objective, work to achieve the organization's goals given adequate information, and balance priorities in a way acceptable to all concerned given the facts of the situation;

(b) needs everyone to be kept informed about what is happening to the task, and when they will be required to do what;

(c) entails the leaders of the lateral groups being seen as co-coordinators, with the most complete knowledge about what is happening to the task and what it will involve in due course, and able to influence events by signaling to the vertical authorities when the project deviates from its plan;

(d) has lateral groups which only need to be a set of nominated individuals concerned with the completion of the task, each knowing who else is involved. The nominated individuals are primarily members of the functional groups, and project work is secondary to their functional work.

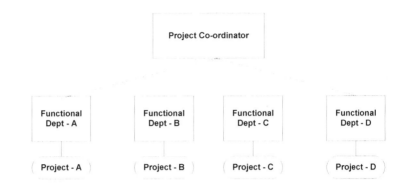

Figure 2-1. Simple Co-ordination Matrix

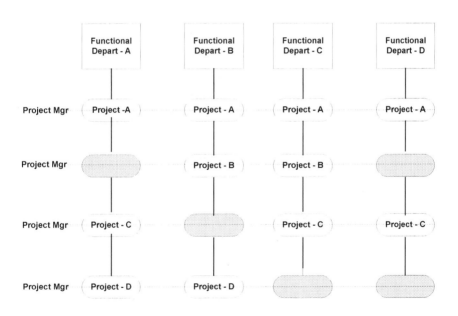

Figure 2-2. Leadership Matrix

(CO-ORDINATION AND LEADERSIP matrix)

CASE STUDY

Let us imagine that a hospital wanted to open a new wing. The construction bid was awarded to ABC Illusions construction company. The scope of the bid entails three separate building segments as part of the new wing. In order to build the wing in the allotted time, it has been decided that each of the building segments will need to be managed by a dedicated Project Manager that will focus and drive each of the wing segments to completion. The planning department has determined that there are only two Bricklayers and one Electrician available that are qualified for this job. The Bricklayers report to a different Functional Manager than the Electricians. After some discussion between the Functional Managers and the Project Manager it is determined that each of the Functional Managers will schedule and share the limited resources for the betterment of the wing completion and profitability of the ABC Illusions construction company. Each Bricklayer and Electrician will report to the Project Manager during the construction of the wings and be allowed to move from project segment to project segment within the wing construction sharing his or her expertise to accomplish the completion of the wing. The Electrical teams' Functional Manager has just received a memo stating that there is new project that was just signed worth three times the revenue as the current hospital project. There is a mandatory project meeting tomorrow that the electrical resource from that Functional manager's team must attend. The Functional manager immediately calls the resource to inform them that their expertise will be needed on this other project as well. The Functional Manager didn't' bother to speak with the Project Manager but instead made the request directly to that Electrician. That resource is now conflicted as to which of these managers instructions to follow. This happens all of the time. This is a point of reflection. Figure 2-1 shows the reporting structure of the Bricklayers and Electrician.

Matrix organizations have an environment that is structured to enable employee resources to be shared across departments similar to the building of the Hospital wing scenario. Employee A may report to a Functional Department manager and be assigned to work on a project for a period. In this situation, that employee now reports to the Project Manager for that project as well as their Functional Department manager; note the dotted line in the organizational chart. The employee now reports to two managers and somewhere in-between the two departments the illusive smoke begins to appear. Which manager do they really report to?

Companies that are in this structure are experiencing the ebbs and flows of this type of structure and are struggling to compensate for the shortcomings while maintaining an appearance of floatation in the annual report. Let us look at the advantages and disadvantages of the ever-flourishing matrix structure that is attributing to some of these issues.

The advantages of the matrix structure are that it encourages the sharing of information and indebt specialization across functional and divisional departments or division within an organization. It reduces the need to hire resources with the same skill set. In short, it saves the company money.

The disadvantages are that this becomes a very confusing and unproductive environment for the employee as well as the division if the two managers are not working on the same goals and objectives. The resource becomes over extended, burned out, and not recognized for the value that they bring to that division and company. Too often, they become viewed as unproductive and excess.

Figure 2-7 Matrix Affect

They are some of the first to be targeted for dismissal when a "restructuring" albeit downsizing is amiss. The matrix structure also exposes the high performers by allowing them to be challenged and exposes the poor performers because they can no longer hide behind the day-to-day maintenance functions of a single project.[7]

Corporations reward managers that produce numbers, not necessarily the managers that play well together. Ironically, the employees working in the matrix organizations are producing those numbers for both managers.

Not all matrix structures are created equally. Variations to the base structure can yield considerably different results, as further examination will attest.

Both the weak and balanced matrix environments have staff reporting to the Functional Department management while the strong matrix environment incorporates a Manager of Project Managers that has project managers reporting to them in place of traditional staff.

Weak Matrix

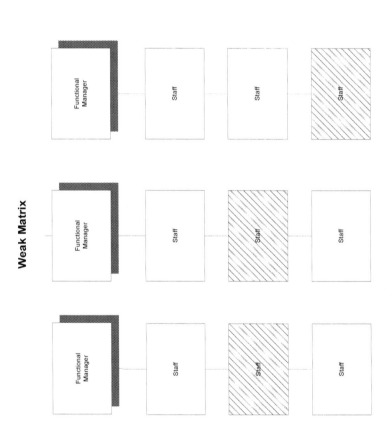

Figure 2-3. Weak Matrix Team

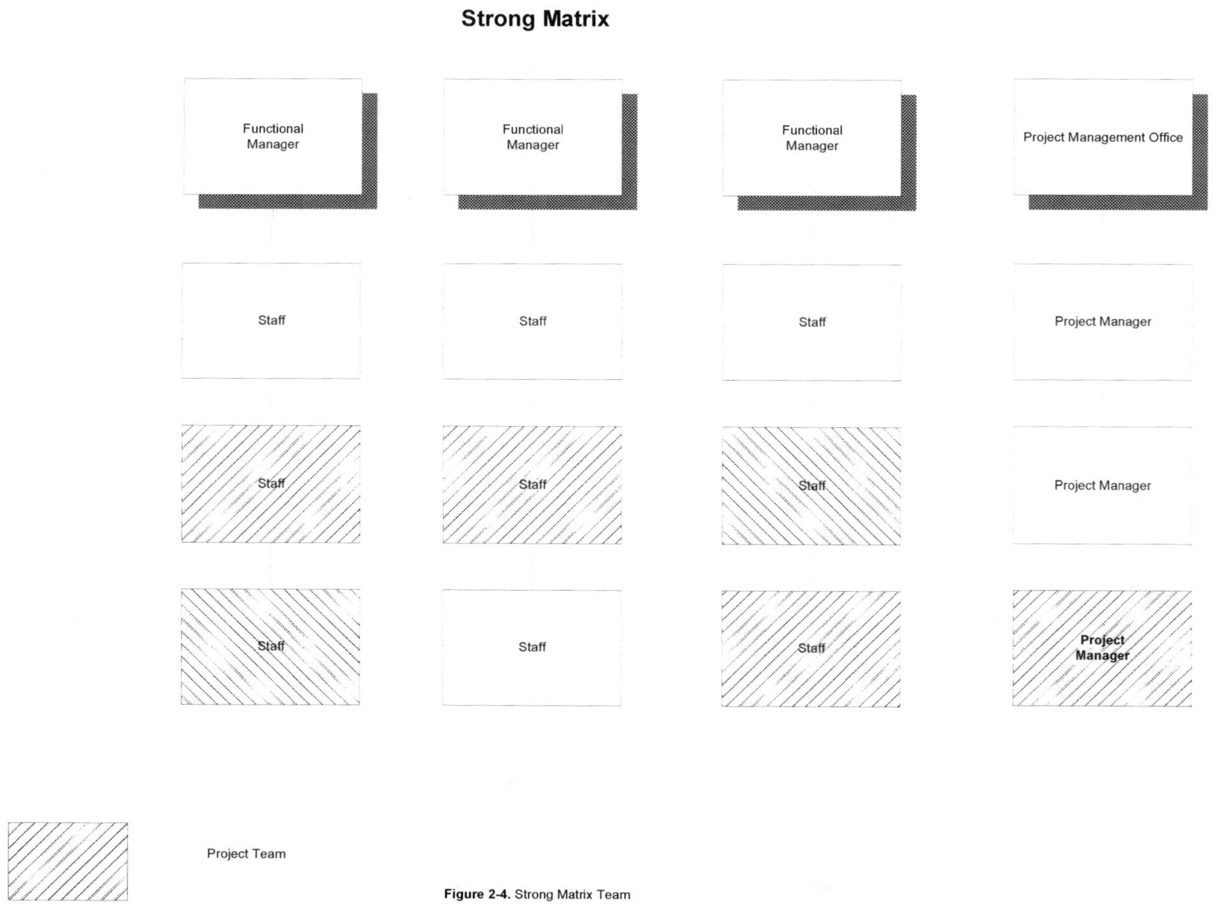

Strong Matrix

Project Management Office	Functional Manager	Functional Manager	Functional Manager
Project Manager	Staff	Staff	Staff
Project Manager	Staff	Staff	Staff
Project Manager	Staff	Staff	Staff

Project Team

Figure 2-4. Strong Matrix Team

Balanced Matrix

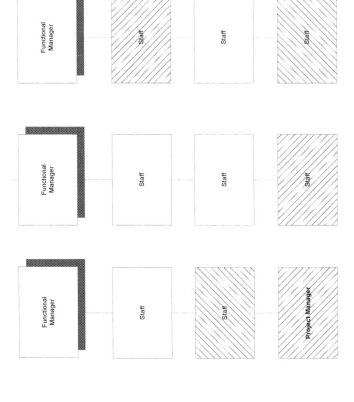

Project Team

Figure 2-5. Balanced Matrix Team

In a Weak/Functional matrix, the project manager assigned is generally a staff member in one of the functional departments. The authority of this employee exists only as an administrator to report the movement of project activity across the functional departments. The Functional Department manager retains control and authority over the resources and the degree to which the project activities are executed. Do not worry, the department is not on fire it is just the beginning of the smoldering effect of the illusion. Just ignore it and the project will never materialize.

In the Balanced/Functional matrix environment an official project manager is assigned the responsibility of overseeing the project and shares power with the functional managers. This system is the most difficult to maintain a balance in power and still achieve the goals and objectives of the corporation. Conflict is unavoidable with dual authority and one of these magicians will undoubtedly disappear. This is where a strong charter from the sponsoring party comes into play. Projects cannot be executed in a vacuum and certainly not without the active direction of the sponsor. This is not the time for the sponsor to be invisible or to entrust that the two will work things out given enough time. What a lovely thought. Surprisingly enough the only time the sponsor emerges is when the smoke from the smoldering fire starts to seep under the door. This event is not an illusion!

In the Strong/Project matrix, the project manager takes on the primary responsibility of the project. This person has other project managers reporting to them as well as key staff resources from various functional management departments on an as-needed basis.

The responsibilities of the resource have to be clearly defined to avoid double and triple booking resource time. Over booking resource is a common mistake in this type of environment and runs the risk of the resource becoming the illusion. Time and task tracking are not an option if resource retention and progress are valued. Some companies utilize resource allocation tracking tools to assist in managing the available time of each resource. We will briefly discuss these tools in a later chapter. In a matrix environment where there are multiple projects in motion and limited key resources available this not an option. The resource availability must be visible and manageable by all involved departments and key personnel. Such is not the case.

CHAPTER 3

THE SHRINKING INTELLECTUAL CAPITAL WAREHOUSE

Where did the focus and discussion on Intellectual Capital go, was that just a term that dovetailed well with Knowledge Management or was it a good idea at the time to acknowledge but did not seem to have the glittery audience appeal to stay as part of the opening act? Many economic discussions will skirt around any acknowledgement that there is a valuable price associated with the retention of Intellectual Capital. The trend today engulfs the immediate need to generate a continued increase in the revenues of companies. Benefits, salaries, working expenditures and as of late, pensions are some of the first items offered as part of the disappearing act on the balance sheet. These same companies are skilled and knowledgeable players in matrix management and seem to have lost the road to the longevity of the profitable existence of the company in the smoldering effect of a matrix organization.

Figure 3-1 Intellectual capital

Intellectual Capital is not an illusion. Maybe you can remember that it was not that long ago during the Y2K panic for resources that obtaining Intellectual Capital was all companies cared about. They needed it to stay in business. Companies were on a quest for a certain type, quantity, and quality of Intellectual Capital and were willing to pay what ever it took to obtain this valued commodity. Today you can hardly go through a day without the news of some major company taking steps to first re-organize, then downsize, finally closing its doors do to lagging profits. Ideas created profits at one time that the company executed on, managed, nurtured, grew and protected. The same ideas that create Intellectual Capital became part of the illusion.

What is Intellectual Capital? More importantly why should any company that wants to stay in business care about it?

Intellectual Capital or Intellectual Asset is the accumulated knowledge that an organization possesses in its people, methodologies, patents, designs, relationships and experience. Any industry whose primary source of revenue is the intangible information that resides with the individual employee relies on Intellectual Capital. What happens when the magic trick does not work? When the Intellectual Capital goes away? Some skeptics would say that it did not exist anyway so nothing happened. They would state that the profits of the company did not decrease this year; after all, we did just have a major reorganization to ensure that the profits would not decline, at least not on paper. Then the skeptics start to notice that they use to be able to get a straight answer, now it just appears that people are showing up for the day with no clear direction and no one can explain what that direction is. The skeptics may even mumble that at some point they use to remember that there was a person or department that understood that direction and actually got something done. What was that department, who was that? Well it appears that someone pulled the trap door behind the curtains in an effort to buy some time while they figured out how their act was going to fit into the strategic plan. They did not understand, how could they, they were just hired straight from one of the top MBA programs and from all accounts nothing here fit into the book models that worked so well on paper in the classroom. Oh, you are wondering about that department that involuntarily left the act. Well they did not leave the act empty handed, they took 32 years of experience with them. They did however leave all of the documentation and "how to" manuals, but the people that picked up the new assignments from the old department could not make it work like before. Forecasts were missed, revenues declined and before long that division was disbanded, the product line dropped and the company was sold off to an off shore company. Oh, was that too fast for you? Well let us back up and try to understand where we were at before the trap door was pulled. Ah yes, the Intellectual Capital discussion.

I submit to those skeptics that question the relevance or existence of Intellectual Capital, the Balance sheets of several major and successful corporations. Please note under "Other Assets" the posting of Intangibles (goodwill, patents). Intangible assets are assets that have no physical existence, yet they hold substantial value to the company. Examples of this would be a patent or exclusive right to produce a product, a trademark or a copyright. Another intangible asset frequently found in the section of the balance sheet is *goodwill.* Goodwill in turn represents the amount by which the price of an acquired company exceeds the fair value of the related net assets acquired. The excess is the value of the company's name and reputation and its customer base, Intellectual Capital and workforce (their expertise, experience, managerial skills etc . . .)

There are several reasons why Intellectual Capital, sometime referred to as Knowledge Management, is virtually ignored in conducting business today.

> **"Managers, Consulting Firms and Information Technologists who design and build the systems for collecting, storing and retrieving knowledge have limited, often inaccurate, views of how people actually use knowledge in their jobs."[8] Most of the learning process, about 70 percent[9], is through social interaction and informal processes, conversations about "what if" and "what do you think about this."**

As the experienced employee, turnover rate continues to rise, voluntarily or not, corporations are starting to realize the significance and impact that Intellectual Capital has on their financial bottom line. Companies are focusing on the development and retention of the best employees . . . Not happening! It would be reasonable to conclude that these employee members posses the Intellectual Capital that will continue to generate the type of revenue and growth that the company expects, or so you would think. The turnover trend costs the corporations millions of dollars each year.

Industry experts site that it cost between one and three times the person's annual salary to replace them. This does not account for the cost of recruiting, training and business down time due to lack of experience and a quality skill set. So SNAP! It's time to wake up. What's a company to do? You got it, they are hiring consultants, and not just any consultants but experienced consultants with guess what—Intellectual Capital. The kind that some other company let go of to create the illusion that the company is doing well. Waving the magic cape the company tells the shareholders not to panic just yet, they tell them that they will let them know when the panic trick is in order. But before the announcement can be made the company goes under, they could no longer produce the products and services that people were buying, oh yes, they let that whole department go a couple of months ago.

Figure 3-2 Intel-Car

"Many firms today have reached the point where they know that they don't know what they used to know, and more importantly need to know in order to be competitive. What happened to that knowledge? Maybe it was washed away in the wave of the downsizing. On the other hand, maybe it was silenced one time too many and walked out the front door. The meeting was a short one when the developers at Ford Motor Company gathered to review what made the Taurus so successful. There was no one left in the company that knew, nor was there any documentation to that effect."[10]

The new, but not so new trick is to get a hold of a deck of those magic cards that hold the Intellectual Capital that companies are clamoring for these days. They are called experienced consultants. There is no magic to this.

CHAPTER 4

VIRTUAL WORKFORCE

What happened to the economy? Well what started as a virtual game turned into a real virtual business. The virtual business gave way to the creation of the virtual work place requiring a virtual workforce. This environment became very popular with businesses giving them the ability to reduce overhead cost and to react quickly to customer demands. This environment also gave the company the competitive edge that is required to survive, or so it was presumed to be. The assumption was holding its own up to the point that it started to morph into a different creature during the creation of all of this virtuality, taking on the form of a virtual economy. Strangely resembles what the world is in right now, a virtual "almost" economy that is vanishing faster than the smoke that created it.

The creation of the virtual workforce, not by mistake, takes on the traits of the disappearance of the brick and mortar, social skills, health attrition, business skills and last but certainly not least, the feeding frenzy into the collapse of the economy.

What does this look like? Well it kind of resembles a sound bite, because that is the form of communication that it takes. Bits and pieces of a string that is almost invisible except for the sound at the other end of the cell phone, BlackBerry™ or SmartPhone™. It looks like an email, a text message, some information on Facebook™ that shouldn't be there.

Figure 4-4 Cell phone "error"

Technology advancements have enabled the virtual workforce to share information but do little to address effective business communication. The emphasis on "gidgets and gadgets" has left the idea of trust and motivational teamwork on the shelf collecting dust.

> *"Trust and teamwork are not the soft matters that one may not attend to.*
> *They are the means by which services and products are delivered"[11]*

Figure 4-5 Cloud Computing gone...

Without the services and products business does not exist. So why is anyone surprised that the economy is in shambles. When technology doesn't work we call a technician in to get it fixed and expect a fix. What have we done to fix the business communications issue? Very little, in fact just the opposite, we have created the workforce vanishing act morphed into the virtual workforce with no plan and very little structure outside of what technology can lend. We have elevated technology concepts such as *cloud computing* to high levels with out the thought of the degradation of the functional business environment. The whole concept that cloud computing is an internet—based environment where resource, software and information are provided to users as needed and on demand. Several issues exist that we have all seen and in most cases felt the effects of these issues, least of all the rise in unemployment. Companies are reacting to the virtual environment that cloud computing creates with the increase in the virtual workforce, out of sight out of mind. Companies have lost site into what it actually takes to run a company, someone on the other end of that cloud is doing the work. Controls are not in place leading to violations in privacy, security, availability, performance and sustainability. This has costs companies tangible billions and intangible trusts, some that can never be repaired.

To further this virtual madness is the access that businesses have to this cyberspace trap door. Interactions in cyberspace through cloud computing gives rise to "Botnet" programs that turn PC's into unwilling zombies.

> *"Zombie PC's can operate in silence, not causing pop-up's or erratic behavior which might alert the user that something is wrong with their system. They lay dormant until the controller of the Botnet needs the resources of his 'Dark Cloud' to cause a denial of service attack, mail millions of spam messages, crack a password, or distribute a crippling exploit."* [12]

Are you asking about the rules again? Of course. The rules of cloud computing are virtual, what else could they be. Where the information exists is in material, or is it? Companies that provide Cloud services control and can, legally or ill legally, monitor communications and data stored between the end user and the host company. Security is always an issue.[13]

> *"Instances such as the secret NSA program, working with AT&T, and Verizon, which recorded over 10 million phone calls between American citizens, causes uncertainty among privacy advocates, and the greater powers it gives to telecommunication companies to monitor user activity."*[14]

History usually repeats itself, so it would behoove us to at least get to understand a little about this environment, where it came from and what it consist of. It is here, and from all accounts, the trap door hinges have not been oiled in a while, not sure if it works anymore. You guessed it, the person that use to do all of the "unimportant" tasks was downsized, so there will be quite a few areas that will cease to work after a while.

> *"In 2007, Google, IBM, and a number of universities embarked on a large scale cloud computing research project. [15] In early 2008, Eucalyptus became the first open source AWS API compatible platform for deploying private clouds. By mid-2008, Gartner saw an opportunity for cloud computing "to shape the relationship among consumers of IT services, those who use IT services and those who sell them",[16] and observed that "organizations are switching from company-owned hardware and software assets to per-use service-based models" so that the "projected shift to cloud computing . . . will result in dramatic growth in IT products in some areas and significant reductions in other areas." [17]*

Now that the rabbit is out of the hat and has created an ever-growing Virtual Workforce family, let us identify some of the characteristics of the various types of Virtual Workforce project teams. The four key variables of a Virtual Workforce are Location, Time Zone, Country and Language. These variables will come into play based on the type of Virtual Workforce.

The Core Team workforce is usually used for smaller projects and the team remains in a centralized location (figure 4-1). The Remote Team workforce is larger and is augmented by subcontractors that may be separated by Time Zone, Countries and/or Languages (figure 4-2).

The third type workforce is a Hybrid / Virtual Team and is used for very large and complex projects. This team consists of the Core Team and the Remote Team that may be further broken down into smaller groups/ teams based on Time Zone, Countries and /or Languages (figure 4-3).

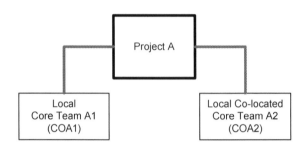

Figure 4-1. Virtual Project Core Team

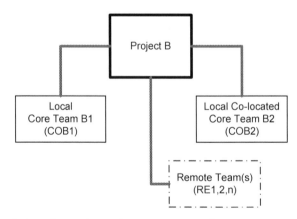

Figure 4-2. Virtual Project Core and Remote Team

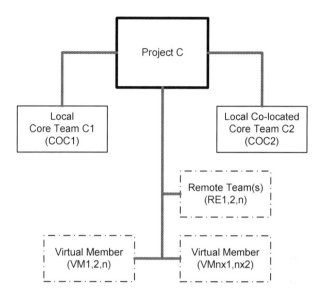

Figure 4-3. Virtual Project Hybrid Team

Nonetheless, the show must go on and the Illusion is real for most businesses. Technology has married cyberspace to create the perfect opportunity to outsource whole departments to offshore companies. Some would say they didn't see this coming, where's the plan?

CHAPTER 5

OFF-SHORE COMPANIES PLAYGROUND

It couldn't get any easier for companies to ship jobs or whole companies to another country. The mass exodus seemed to have picked up the pace after the Y2K balloon started to drift back into the earth's stratosphere, or maybe we just had more free time on our hands to notice when jobs started to vanish. Vanish in the sense that whole departments were not just moved to another state but also physically removed from ANY state.

Figure 5-1 World from afar

CASE STUDY

One such company decided to join the exodus march, first starting with the "back-office" group. The "back-office" group were key administrators for field support that performed installations for high profile customers. The operations where moved to Costa Rica in a cost savings frenzy. What is the backup plan you ask in the event that things went "south" (no pun intended)? If there was a backup plan, it was a well-kept secret. Service took a noise dive, partial shipments were sent or no shipments at all. Completion milestones were strained, budgets were destroyed because of additional hours required to physically "double—dip" on sites that had to be re-visited with the correct hardware that could have been installed during the initial site install. Key customers were witnessing the ciaos and wondered what was going on and without being said the implication was "oh-by-the-way, sorry to hear, see that you are having transition difficulties but we are still expecting the project to be finished on time". Instead of saving money the cost were staggering. As a result, several of the key accounts were moved back to the United States.

According to Ocraworldwide, an Offshore services company, the reason for going off-shore include:[18]

> ➢ Free remittance of profits and capital
> ➢ Access to top-rated debt history jurisdictions
> ➢ Access to tax treaties
> ➢ Security of property rights
> ➢ Accessing low cost areas
> ➢ Banking privacy
> ➢ Availability of offshore experts

> Access to foreign insurance and reinsurance
> Enhanced privacy
> Customs and duty exemptions
> Exchange convertibility
> Government cooperation
> Fair treatment
> Territorial taxation on foreign income
> Fewer restrictions
> Sanctity of contracts
> Foreign investment inducements
> Tested legal systems
> Higher yields and returns
> The availability of sophisticated banking facilities
> Reduced taxation
> The search for political stability

According to Ocraworldwide the principle application of Offshore companies are:

> Trading
> Investment
> Holding
> Financing
> Professional services or consultancy
> Patent, royalty and copyright holding
> Ship management and yacht owning
> Personal and corporate tax planning

Did we cover about everything in this scene or is there more? There is always more if you stay for the second act. Here we go.

The lists are extensive but the bottom line, as we all know, is to cut cost. The question is just how far a company should take this cost cutting exercise before the company is paralyzed and ineffective to the point where it has to close the doors.

CASE STUDY

This is a typical, but true story that you have either read, heard about, or have been a part of the story line. There was a company that was successful that underwent IT leadership changes with one of the goals being cost-cutting tactics. Within a few years, the once productive IT department could not deliver projects on time and sometimes projects were not delivered at all. Employees were assigned to multiple projects sometimes over allocated by two to three hundred percent. The employees didn't know which projects to work on and just assumed that the projects wouldn't be successful anyway.

One of the most important business driving projects was part of the project summary listing. The Senior Management believed the "green" status reports that they received each week from the consulting company. This particular vendor had been selected primarily because they fit within the companies cost-cutting model that they had adopted. The reason that the company could bid so low was because of their off-shore affiliations with coding and software production. The non-management employees knew that the project was not green and in fact, it was in trouble. Nevertheless, the Senior Management refused to listen and had complete trust in the consulting company. Sure enough the system did not work. The key production line product was delayed, orders were missed, invoices did not go out on time and eventually the company had to close its doors.[19] Doesn't this sound familiar?

CASE STUDY

During the last few years, the housing market jumped on stage disguised as the dance partner of the financial institutions for the beginning of the second act. One very large financial institution was a participant of sending business offshore surely for financial purposes. On paper it had to look like a good idea until the trap door opened off cue and the financial institute had all spotlights on it. A customer called 911 to report that someone was trying to break into her home. Apparently, the financial institution had given a locksmith company instructions to change all of her locks. She never received notification of the foreclosure. The financial institution was sending the foreclosure documents to off shore companies for processing. The companies were bypassing procedures and were processing the documents. Several other financial institutions were put under the microscope for similar practices and all foreclosure proceedings were stopped pending procedural investigations. Anyone's guess as to how much that all cost. Where are the savings?

Figure 5-2 The Housing Market

Adding to the smoldering economy is the fact that ***previously high-paying jobs in manufacturing have gone the way of the Edsel. U.S. factories lost 3 million jobs from 2000 to 2004, jobs that did not return during the boom leading up to the recession, along with another 2.2 million from 2007 to 2010. Those are unlikely to come back, as well. Manufacturing jobs were 20 percent of private-sector payrolls in 1990, 15 percent in 2000, and just over 10 percent in April 2010. Large multinational corporations have cut 2.9 million U.S. jobs over the decade, while adding 2.4 million workers to their overseas operations.***[20]

How do we fix the economy if the jobs are never coming back? Maybe they won't come back, that may be true and there is nothing that we can do about what's already happened. What we can do something about is the here and now and prevent more jobs from leaving the country starting with the efficiencies of how companies are executing their Strategic Plan.

CHAPTER 6

PORTFOLIO TO PROGRAM TO PROJECT VANISHING ACT

Why are so many companies struggling, where should we begin? Is it because of the technologies that allow businesses to send jobs to off-shore companies, creating virtual staffs, devaluation and loss of Intellectual Capitol, or is it just dysfunctional matrix organizations?

Many companies have seen what should have been a portfolio of products and services handled as defunct individual projects. They want to take on projects but do not want to step up to the plate to see them through in the fashion that they should. Companies don't realize that there has got to be a Sponsor that has a big stick and doesn't mind using it with unpopular projects, they are "ugly", some more than others. There are no magic applications or tools that will substitute for good business practices with sound planning and some foresight as to where the company is going. How about a little strategic planning or just plain ole planning period! What a thought. Companies buy Project Portfolio Management tools all the time in search of that magic bullet that will instantly turn the company around or somehow skirt around the fact that there was no strategic plan in place for the business. What adds insult to injury is that these same companies will only implement one or two of the ten packaged modules and forego the necessary training to implement the two modules that they purchased. Therefore, you ask what happens next. Well in the case of the Project and Portfolio Management tool, the company came to realize that the modules did not work as anticipated so someone made the command decision to get rid of the modules and try something else. Eventually the portfolio began to vanish one project at a time along with the business. The fact remains that it should be the Business strategy governing the Product strategy driving the IT strategy, in that order.

Companies by and large do want control over their projects and portfolios but hesitate and tread softly towards implementation due to the traditional lengthy and expensive implementation path for PPM solutions.[21] Today several companies offer PPM solutions that in fact address these concerns. They offer flexible implementation strategies that shorten the implementation period from months to weeks. These vendors have also recognized that companies are looking for prepackaged solutions that include training and support services that will allow them to see a return on investment in a short timeframe. The third consideration is creating a positive user experience by creating adaptable workflows and enabling work-management to be configured to support a wider range of maturity levels.[22]

Several key PPM tools were evaluated in the Forrester study. The following are some of the strengths and weaknesses of each of these PPM tools for evaluation.

Types of Project Portfolio Management Tools

	AtTask	Clarity	HP-PPM	MS Enterprise	Primavera
CURRENT OFFERING	2.99	4.55	4.38	3.49	4.43
Core functionality	3.70	4.71	4.60	4.04	4.28
Advanced functionality	2.68	4.49	4.29	3.25	4.49
STRATEGY	3.34	4.80	4.44	4.44	4.80
Product strategy	3.15	5.00	4.60	4.60	5.00
Corporate strategy	5.00	3.00	3.00	3.00	3.00
Cost	5.00	4.00	4.50	4.50	3.00
MARKET PRESENCE	3.91	3.52	3.75	2.69	3.28
Installed base	4.20	3.80	3.80	3.80	4.20
Revenue	5.00	3.00	3.00	0.00	4.20
Revenue growth	5.00	3.00	3.00	0.00	3.00
Systems Integrators	2.00	5.00	5.00	5.00	5.00
Employees	3.40	2.60	4.00	3.70	1.50
Technology partners	2.50	5.00	4.00	5.00	2.50

Note:(1) All scores are based on a scale of 0 (weak) to 5 (strong)
resource management, demand management, portfolio management, and
financial management capabilities.

Figure 6-1 The Forrester Wave ™. Business-Driven Project Portfolio Management, Q4 2009

*AtTask—AtTask

Strength—Easy to implement and is user friendly. Allows user to work from the portfolio level to the project and activity management level. It is an economical offering for organizations that want to get started with a PPM model.

Weakness—Activities will need to be monitored for completion if not integrated into the organizations business systems for notifications on status.

*CA Clarity (formerly NIKU)

Strength—Is strong in IT project delivery processes such as requirements management and release planning.

Is best suited for mature IT organizations but can be adapted to the maturing organizations.

Weakness—Should be integrated into the organizations project workflow systems such as time keeping and finance systems.

*HP Project and Portfolio Management Center

Strength—Provides depth in managing various types of IT projects. Offers executive visibility into the impact and cost of IT investments.

Weakness—Is suited for complex larger IT management needs can be very expensive. Not recommended if the implementation modules are not completely functional and integrated with the company time keeping, resource and finance systems.

*MS Project Enterprise

Strength—Utilizes the Enterprise Project Management tool along with the SharePoint platform to allow for PPM functions from strategic planning through collaborative efforts from individual contributors.

Weakness—Requires formal training to become a functional tool. Can be expensive to implement depending on the size of the organization.

*Oracles Primavera

Strength—Meets the needs of mature, project-focused organizations. Offers end-to-end life cycle planning.

Weakness—Is best suited for business-driven projects with extensive planning requirements. Works well in an SDLC or Waterfall environment.

*   *   *   *   *   *   *   *   *

"On Average, Strategy Is Executed to Plan Only Fifty-Six Percent of the Time."[23] The ladder to the C-Level Executive Decision Makers goes from Projects to Programs to the Portfolios. Well it makes sense that if the projects are not representative and do not feed into the definition of what the portfolio is then yes most of the companies will fail, and they are failing. If projects are being executed off shore and they either do not know what the strategic plan is for the portfolio then yes most of the companies will fail, and they are failing. The question is how to stop the portfolio vanishing act. A good start is to understand what makes up a basic portfolio. From that stance, the projects can be selected and fashioned to support the portfolio thereby supporting the strategic plan.

First thing first, know what the strategic plan is. Sounds simple but too often IT projects are in motion and the CEO is unaware of their progress, uncertain of their objectives, and unengaged in their challenges.[24] In order for projects to be successful, they must follow the basic Project Portfolio Management standards by capturing:

- Standard definitions for Projects
- Total cost and Benefits estimates
- Labor and Non-Labor resource estimates
- Stakeholder Impacts
- Measurable success criteria
- Return on Investment

- External Dependencies
- Stakeholder Inputs

If projects are consistent with these criteria then maybe there is a chance that the success rate of the projects can be improved and the companies can keep the doors open longer, start to grow again and hire a few people to improve the Economy. What an idea!

Let us talk strategy.

CHAPTER 7

THE STRATEGIC PLAN

In the beginning, there was an idea. The idea was to become a profitable company. Simple enough, but the question is how? So let us talk about strategies. There are basically three different strategies to consider when creating a portfolio: Corporate Strategy, Business Strategy and Functional Strategy.[25]

Corporate Strategy

Corporate—Level Strategies scope encompasses the entire company. These strategies determine which product or service markets to compete in, which geographic regions to operate in, how cash, staffing, equipment and other resources are distributed. Corporate—Level Strategies address product and geographic market diversification. The Boston Consulting Group matrix does a nice job in simplifying how to access the performance of products or services.[23] Each product or service is categorized into one of four groups:

Group one are New Business, these are called Question Marks. They basically use cash for market research, test marketing and advertising and do not produce any revenue.

Group two are high market share and high growth market they are called Stars. This group produces a high influx of cash but it also uses a large quantity of money to sustain growth.

Group three are high market share and low growth they are called Cash cows. This group is well established and well recognized. The strategy for this group is to invest little and use the monies to invest in the Stars or Question Marks.

Group four are low market share and low growth; they are called Dogs. This group should be closed down and the monies used on Stars or Question Marks.

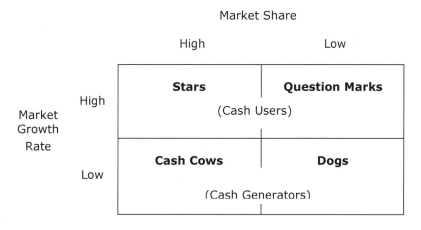

Figure 7-1 BCG Model of Portfolio Analysis

Once the characteristics of the strategy are identified, the company can proceed with a plan to include or not include that product or services. The next step is to determine what type strategy the group falls into, growth, retrenchment or stability.[26] *Growth* strategies are designed to expand the organization and are measured by sales, profits, product mix, market coverage, market share or some other accounting mix. *Stability* strategies are just a continuation of existing strategies. The company is basically satisfied with the growth rate and profits. The last strategy is *Retrenchment*. This is the strategy that companies as of late are executing on. It generally requires many pink slips being handed out, the discontinuation of a product line or service and the possibility of restructuring through bankruptcy actions or liquidation of the organization.

Business Strategy

Business-level strategies are somewhat like Corporate—level strategies because they focus on overall performance only in one area of the company. At the business level there can be multiple divisions each responsible for its own profit and loss. They have a certain synergy and need to stay focused and aligned with the corporate strategy at all times. This requires clarity of the Strategic plan to an execution state in overall cost leadership, differentiation and market identification.

Functional Strategy

Functional-level strategies support and feed into the Business-level strategies project by project. Each project should be aligned to the goals of the firm and in support of the overall portfolio. Each project should support the overall mission statement. "The firm will be recognized in the market we serve for providing a broad range of the highest quality technology services to quality clients throughout the country."

- Our strength and stability will be manifested by our employee's commitment to the Firm ahead of their individual interests.

- In effectively fulfilling our intense commitment to our clients and our Firm, we will integrate our diverse skills, perspective and background within a collegial environment.

Each project should be able to point directly to and in support of the company goals for that year. Does this project support-

- The increase in gross revenues
- The improvement of client base
- The restructuring of the management base
- Infrastructure and communication application network that will support a national and local group structure.
- Provide and infrastructure for company growth
- Delivery of system availability anytime, anywhere.

In order to achieve these goals each project should be executed utilizing a repeatable project process. The standard project process generally consist of nine stages: (1)Strategy, (2) Requirements, (3) Design, (4) Development / Construction, (5) Integration & Testing, (6) Documentation & Training, (7) Implementation, (8) Operations / Acceptance, (9) On-going Support.

Let us examine each of these stages in some detail in the following chapters.

Each project usually begins as a "request". A request becomes a project once it has been determined that (1) the project fits within the company's long-term strategic plan; (2) the project meets the criteria outlined in the tactical plan and (3) the project fills a true business need or in some way enhances the business. These factors are determined through a structured business analysis process that evaluates requests and then transitions the request into a formal project. The Illusion Specialist Company LLC will take us through this process.

CHAPTER 8

THE ILLUSION SPECIALIST COMPANY LLC.

The Illusion Specialist Company LLC determined that it could increase its profit margin for the magic supplies that it produced by 6% if it could somehow increase the number of order calls that it could take without hiring more people. The request was emailed to the IT department who in turn set up a formal meeting to discuss the requirements. Everyone agreed that this was a worthwhile project to evaluate, but where to begin? From experience, the IT manager knew that:

- 31 percent of all software projects are canceled before they are completed (a waste of $81 billion).

- 53 percent of projects cost 189 percent of their original estimate.

- In large companies, 9 percent of projects are on time and within budget.

- In small companies, 16 percent of projects are on time and within budget.

- The three top impairment factors are (1) Lack of user input=12.8%,(2)Incomplete requirements and specifications=12.3%,(3)Changing requirements and specifications=11.8%.[27]

The IT manager was determined not to let these factors happen to this project so he hired an experienced Business Analyst and Project Manager to spear head this effort.

Figure 8-2 Project Team

Well we know that this project was in line with the strategic plan, to grow this sector of the business by 6%. So next steps? Of course to gather the Requirements, the right way. Requirements are used in several ways—project scoping, cost estimating, budgeting, project scheduling, software design, software testing, documentation and training manuals.[28] The purpose of the Requirements Stage is to create a clear picture of the proposed project by gathering, analyzing and modeling the specifications of the Business Functional and the Technical requirements.

The following Project Process Model will serve as our guide for this project.

Project Team Members

- Sponsor
- Project Manager
- Business Analyst
- Quality Analyst
- Architect
- Developer
- Infrastructure Engineer
- Help Desk Support
- Operations

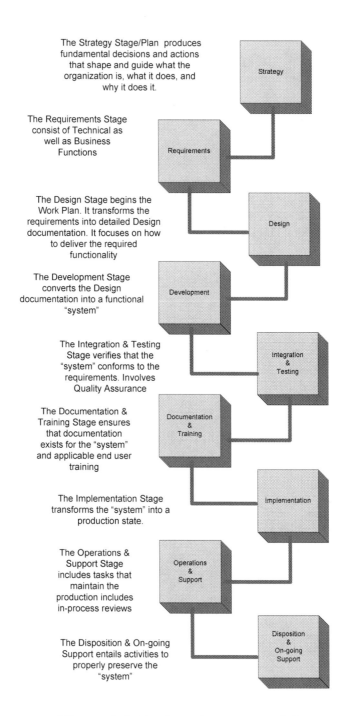

Figure 8-1. Project Process Model

CHAPTER 9

REQUIREMENTS STAGE

What is a requirement and why is it so important to accurately document each requirement? Written requirements address the question of What needs to happen not How it should happen. How it happens is in the Design Stage. Requirements need to be direct, they cannot be ambiguous and they must be verifiable in the Testing Stage. For example: The system must be easy to use for new office users and organized in such a way that user errors are minimized to no more than 2 per day. Why are accurate requirements so important? Remember the statics that the IT manager pointed out in the previous chapter? Those are real to this day. Companies just cannot seem to get it right because they fail to follow the rules, garbage in expensive garbage out! Document those requirements!!

The Requirements Stage consists of Technical as well as Business Function requirement specifications tasks as the following process flow shows.

Inputs

1. Output documentation (SOW) from the Strategy Stage
2. Assignment of Project Manager
3. Selection of Project Team participants
4. Project Plan Outline
5. Project Kick-off

Process—list of tasks to accomplish this stage

1. Information Gathering
   a. Identify Core group of Users and Areas of Analysis
   b. Interview / survey the Users
   c. Analyze Current Systems
   d. Refine Cost Estimate
   e. Refine Risk Analysis—if required

2. Define Requirements
   a. Develop Problem List
   b. Determine Functional Requirements
   c. Determine Technical Requirements
   d. Determine Training Requirements
   e. Develop high level process flowchart (Case Diagram)

3. Acceptance Test Definition
   a. Sponsor review and approval
   b. End-User review and approval

Outputs—list of deliverables, tasks resulting from this stage

1. Detailed resource requirements with cost estimate
2. Technical documentation of System with impact analysis
3. Training scope and requirements
4. Functional (end-user) requirements
5. Technical requirements
6. Refined Project Plan
7. Acceptance Test Plan

The *Inputs and Outputs* of the process are self-explanatory. This *Process* is where tasks are usually missed.

(1a) The first step is to identify all stakeholders. End users represent a class of stakeholders, but by no means do they represent the interests of the whole organization. Other classes of stakeholders can come from finance and accounting, procurement, and IT, as well as from other departments or organizations that directly or indirectly support or benefit from the project.[29]

(1b) The second step is to interview / survey the stakeholders. This can be performed utilizing several techniques such as one-on-one meetings, questionnaires, and storyboarding or Joint Application Development (JAD) sessions.

(1c) The third step is to analyze the current systems that will be affected. Find out what type of Application Programming Interfaces (API) will be required and how the new system will affect the existing systems.

(1d)   The fourth step is to do a cost benefit analysis. Obviously you will need to know how much this new system is going to cost and if it is going to provide the cost savings and function to the company portfolio as anticipated.

(1e)   The fifth step is to refine the risk assessment, as required.

Once the needs and features of the system are identified, it is time to define the requirements. Requirements need to address Contract obligations, Standards or Needs of the End Users and they are either functional (Use cases) or non-functional.

Functional requirements provide a complete description of what the system will do. They should address both the business aspect as well as the technical aspect of the system. A use case defines the workflow of the system from the users' perspective. There is generally no technical depiction of the system. A workflow analysis can be performed to capture these types of requirements. The technical aspect of the functional requirements is captured from engineers, developers and programmers as a separate document in conjunction with the Use cases document.

Non-functional requirements represent properties and constraints of the system. They should address the performance or quality of the performance of the system. Non-functional requirements are organized into five categories:[30]

1. Usability
2. Reliability
3. Performance
4. Supportability
5. Security

Usability describes the ease with which the system can be learned or used. A typical usability requirement may state:

- The system should allow novice users to install and operate it with little or no training.

- The end user shall be able to place an order within thirty seconds.

- The end user shall be able to access any page within four seconds.

Reliability describes the degree to which the system must work for users. Specifications for reliability typically refer to availability, mean time between failures, and mean time to repair, accuracy, and maximum acceptable bugs. For example:

- The system shall meet the terms of a Service Level Agreement.

- The mean time to failure shall be at least four months.

Performance specifications typically refer to response time, transaction throughput, and capacity. For example:

- All Web pages must download within three seconds during an average load, and five seconds during a peak load.

- While executing a search, the system must be able to display 500 search results per page.

Supportability refers to the software's ability to be easily modified or maintained to accommodate typical usage or change scenarios. For instance, in our help desk example, how easy should it be to add new applications to the support framework? Here are some examples of supportability requirements:

- The system shall allow users to create new workflows without the need for additional programming.

- The system shall allow the system administrator to create and populate tax tables for the upcoming tax year.

Security refers to the ability to prevent and/or forbid access to the system by unauthorized parties. Some examples of security requirements are:

- User authentication shall be via the corporate Single Sign on system.

- Only authorized payroll administrators shall be permitted to access employee pay information.

Here is a list of good requirement characteristics:

1. **Complete**—The requirement has no missing information or as much information as is known at the beginning of the project.

2. **Unambiguous**—It must be expressed in objective facts not opinions. There are no vague subjects, adjectives, prepositions or verbs and there are no negative statements.

3. **Consistent**—The requirement cannot contradict another requirement.

4. **Traceable**—The requirement must be able to be tracked back to the business need.

5. **No design information**—There is no design information in the requirements. Requirements are stated as *what* the system will do not *how* the system functions.

6. **Verifiable**—The requirement must be able to be inspected, demonstrated, tested or analyzed.

Well-documented requirements are the key to the success of any project. If you cannot identify it then you cannot build it. So now, we are ready to take our documented requirements to the Design Stage and sequential Supporting Stages.

CHAPTER 10

SUPPORTING STAGE ACTS

Design or not to Design, should that be the question? Assuming the requirements are good, continue to the Design stage.

Design Stage

The purpose of the Design Stage is three fold. First, to create and validate the end user's functional specifications. The second objective is to take the functional specifications and create technical and internal views of the system/application. The last objective of this stage is to create a transition plan to cut over to the new system/application.

Design elements describe the desired application and / or infrastructure features in detail, and generally include functional hierarchy diagrams, screen layout diagrams, tables of business rules, business process diagrams, pseudo code, and a complete entity-relationship diagram with a full data dictionary. These design elements are intended to describe the application and / or infrastructure in sufficient detail that skilled developers or engineers can develop the software or infrastructure environment with minimal additional input design.[31]

The following is the proposed process flow to create the required design elements:

Inputs

1. Output documentation from the Requirements Stage
2. Assignment of project tasks
3. Develop RFI/RFP documentation (include a vendor rating list)—if applicable
4. Select Vendor—if applicable

Process—list of tasks to accomplish this stage

1. Initiate Design
2. Create and Document the Application or Infrastructure Architecture
3. Decide on Package Selection—if applicable
4. Decide on Vendor Management process—if applicable
5. Create and Document Functional Specifications
6. Create and Document Technical Specifications
7. Create and Document Manual Procedures
8. Create and Document Database or Network environment
9. Create and Document Operational environment
10. Design the Network environment
11. Size the System based on the Design
12. Identify the Hardware and associated Cost
13. Identify the Software and associated Cost
14. Identify Licensing cost—if applicable for upgrade
15. Create details for End-User Training and documentation

16. Create details for IS Training and documentation
17. Create Conversions—if applicable
18. Develop the Transition / Migration Plan
    a. Identification of pilot groups, time durations, etc.
    b. Installation Plan
    c. Unit Test Plan
    d. System Test Plan
    e. Functional Test Plan
    f. Rollout schedules

Outputs—list of deliverables, tasks resulting from this stage

1. Transition Plan / Migration
2. Detailed Technical Specifications
3. Detailed Functional Specifications
4. Vendor selection criterion rating document—if applicable
5. Technical review and approval
6. End-User review and approval

Development Stage

The purpose of the Development Stage is to create system and application functions that conform to the functional and technical design specifications while controlling the expenditure of time and money.

The following tasks elements are recommended to successfully develop the system or application:

Inputs

1. Output documentation from the Design Stage

2. Review / Confirmation of Programming estimates from Programmers

Process—list of tasks to accomplish this Stage

1. Initiate Development
2. Develop System Functions
3. Develop Applications
4. Develop Conversions
5. Hardware Implementation
6. Develop Training Documentation
7. Perform Unit Testing
8. Perform System Testing

Outputs—list of deliverables, tasks resulting from this stage

1. Final Product is ready for piloting
2. Draft Training Documentation
3. Training Scenario
4. Training Schedule
5. Send out rollout notification
   a. Local implementation schedule
   b. Training schedule

Integration & Testing / Documentation & Training Stage

The purpose of this stage is to test the system and the associated documentation in a controlled environment. The testing must verify that the "system" conforms to the requirements. This stage also involves Quality Assurance for the system as well as the associated documentation.

The following task elements are recommended at a minimum for a successful Pilot at this Stage:

Inputs

1. Documentation from the Development Stage

Process—list of task to accomplish this Stage

1. Initiate Documentation and Training
2. Finalize End—User Documentation
3. Finalize Technical Documentation
4. Finalize Training Curriculum
5. Perform Training (Core Group initially trained for Pilot testing)
    a. Core Group End-User training
    b. Core Group IS Staff training
    c. End-User training
    d. IS training

Outputs—list of deliverables, tasks resulting from this stage

1. Trained Core Group End-User's and IS Staff
2. Trained End-User and IS Staff

Implementation Stage

The Implementation Stage transforms the "system" into a production state. The purpose of the Implementation Stage is to give the end users the essential time required to test the functional and technical accuracy of the system / application by executing the Acceptance Test Plan.

The following element tasks are essential to put the "system" into production:

Inputs

1. Acceptance Test Plan
2. Transition / Migration Plan
   a. Installation Plan
   b. Unit Test Plan
   c. System Test Plan
   d. Functional Test Plan

Process—list of task to accomplish this stage

1. Install Software
   a. System
   a. Workstation

2. Acceptance Test Support
   a. IS Technical Staff
   b. End-User

3. Perform Conversion
4. Prepare Final Rollout, Schedule, Checklist and Training Schedule
5. Cut-Over

Outputs—list of deliverables, tasks resulting from this stage

1. End-User approval
2. IS / Regional approval
3. Sponsor approval
4. Complete Transition / Migration Plan
5. Execute Rollout, Schedule, Checklist and Training Schedule

Operations & Support Stage

The Operations and Support Stage includes tasks that maintain the "system" production state, this includes in-process reviews. The purpose of this state is to provide a structured environment with procedures that address the on-going activities after cut over to the new system / application.

The following element tasks list the by-products of this stage:

Inputs

1. Job logs
2. History logs
3. Timings
4. Requirements Document
5. End-User input

Process-list of task to accomplish this stage

1. Installation Follow-up
2. Facilities Management—system, facilities
3. Problem Management—Help Desk
4. Change Management—modifications and enhancements
5. Maintenance

Outputs—list of deliverables, tasks resulting from this stage

1. Help Desk Procedures
2. User & System documentation (revised)
3. Back up and Recovery Plan (revised)

Disposition & On-going Support Stage

The Disposition and On-going Support Stage entails activities to properly preserve the "system". The purpose of this state is to examine the project elements to determine what areas were executed well and which areas need improvement.

The following are the element tasks that compose this Stage:

Inputs

1. Work Plan
2. Weekly Status Reports
3. Meeting notes / Communications
4. Change Request
5. Issues

Process-list of task to accomplish this stage

1. Assess the overall project success
2. Identify tasks that were done well
3. Identify tasks that require improvement

Outputs-list of deliverables, tasks resulting from this stage

1. Documentation for Project improvement and on-going support

CHAPTER 11

PROJECT METHODOLOGIES

After scanning the vast sea of failed projects, you quickly realize that there is a common theme, there is little to no structure or clear direction in execution. Many companies do not realize that in order for projects to be successful there has to be clarity in the form of execution. The clarity of this form should be dictated based on the nature of the project; one size does not fit all projects. There are several types of execution forms that come under the heading of "Methodologies". Many of them will utilize varying degrees of the element Stages that we have reviewed. Knowing what to use and when are key skills and usually these skills only come with experience, there are no successful shortcuts. So let us discuss some of the more popular "Methodologies".

Agile

Agile methods break tasks into small increments with minimal planning, and do not directly involve long-term planning. Iterations are short time frames (time boxes) that typically last from one to four weeks. Iterations involve a team working through a full software development cycle including planning, requirements analysis, design, coding, unit testing, and acceptance testing when a working product is demonstrated to stakeholders. This minimizes overall risk and allows the project to adapt to changes quickly. Stakeholders produce documentation as required. An iteration may not add enough functionality to warrant a market release, but the goal is to have an available release (with minimal bugs) at the end of each iteration. Multiple iterations may be required to release a product or new features.[32]

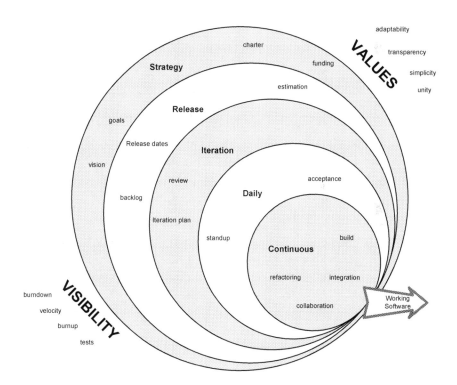

Figure 16-1. Agile Development - Accelerated Delivery Model

Agile methods emphasize face-face communication over written documents when the team is all in the same location. Most agile teams work in a single open office (called a bullpen), which facilitates such communications. Team size is typically small (5-9 people) to simplify team communication and team collaboration.[33] Each team will contain a customer representative appointed by the stakeholders to act on their behalf. At the end of each iteration, stakeholders and the customer representative review progress and re-evaluate priorities with a view to optimizing the return on investment (ROI) and ensuring alignment with customer needs and company goals[34]— referencing back to the "Strategic Plan", what an idea!

SDLC

The System Development Life Cycle (SDLC) framework provides a sequence of activities for system designers and developers to follow. It consists of a set of steps or phases in which each phase of the SDLC uses the results of the previous one.[35] A Systems Development Life Cycle (SDLC) adheres to important phases that are essential for developers, such as planning, analysis, design, and implementation as noted:[36]

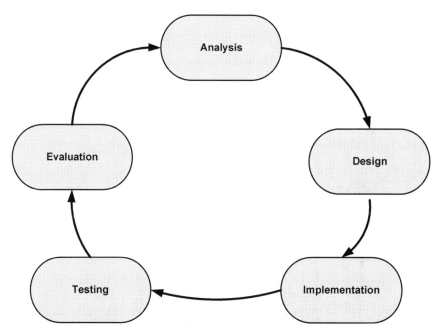

Figure 16-2. (SDLC) Systems (Software) Development Life Cycle Model

- **Project evaluation, feasibility study:** Establishes a high-level view of the intended project and determines its goals.

- **System analysis, requirements definition**: Divides project goals into defined functions and operation of the intended application and analyzes end-user information needs.

- **System design**: Describes desired features and operations in detail, including screen layouts, business rules, process diagrams, pseudo code and other documentation.

- **Implementation**: The real code is written here.

- **Integration and testing**: Brings all the pieces together into a special testing environment, then checks for errors, bugs and interoperability.

- **Acceptance, installation, deployment**: The final stage of initial development, where the software is put into production and runs actual business.

- **Maintenance**: What happens during the rest of the software's life: changes, correction, additions, and moves to a different computing platform and more. This step can go on indefinitely.[37]

Waterfall

The Waterfall model is a sequential design process, often used in software development processes, in which progress is seen as flowing steadily downwards through the phases of Conception, Initiation, Analysis, Design, Construction, Testing, Production/Implementation and Maintenance.[38]

The waterfall development model originates in the manufacturing and construction industries: highly structured physical environments in which after-the-fact changes are prohibitively costly, if not impossible.[39]

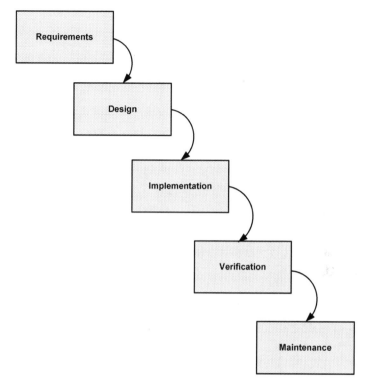

Figure 16-3. Waterfall Model

Waterfall is probably the oldest of the methodologies and bares a fare amount of criticism because of its inflexible nature. Many argue the waterfall model is a bad idea in practice—believing it impossible for any non-trivial project to finish a phase of a software product's lifecycle perfectly before moving to the next phase and learning from them. For example, clients may not know exactly what requirements they need before reviewing a working prototype and commenting on it. They may change their requirements constantly. Designers and programmers may have little control over this. If clients change their requirements after the design is finalized, the design must be modified to accommodate the new requirement. This effectively means invalidating a good deal of working hours, which means increased cost, especially if a large amount of the projects resources has already been invested in Big Design Up Front. Doesn't this sound familiar?[40]

Designers may not be aware of future implementation difficulties when writing a design for an unimplemented software product. That is, it may become clear in the implementation phase that a particular area of program functionality is extraordinarily difficult to implement. In this case, it is better to revise the design than persist in a design based on faulty predictions, and that does not account for the newly discovered problems.[41]

Even without any such changes to the specifications during implementation, there is the option either to start a new project from scratch or to continue some already existing design. The waterfall methodology can be used for continuous enhancement, even for existing software, originally from another team. In the case where the analyst fails to capture the customer requirements correctly, the resulting impact on the following phases (mainly the coding) still can be tamed by this methodology, in practice: A challenging job for a QA team.[42]

JAD

The Joint Application Design (JAD) process includes approaches for enhancing user participation, expediting development and improving the quality of specifications. It consists of a workshop where "knowledge" workers and IT specialists meet, sometimes for several days, to define and review the business requirements for the system. The attendees include high-level management officials who will ensure the product provides the needed reports and information at the end. This acts as a management process which allows Corporate Information Services (IS) departments to work more effectively with users in a shorter time frame. In the end, this process will result in a new information system that is feasible and appealing to both the designers and end users.[43]

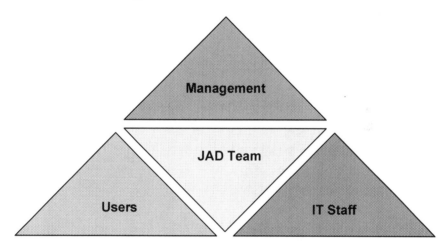

Figure 16-4. (JAD) Joint Application Design (Development)

Key participants:[44]

Executive Sponsor: The executive who charters the project, the system owner. They must be high enough in the organization to be able to make decisions and provide the necessary strategy, planning and direction.

Subject Matter Experts: These are the business users, the IS professionals, and the outside experts that will be needed for a successful workshop. This group is the backbone of the meeting; they will drive the changes.

Facilitator/Session Leader: Chairs the meeting and directs traffic by keeping the group on the meeting agenda. The facilitator is responsible for identifying those issues that can be solved as part of the meeting and those which need to be assigned at the end of the meeting for follow-up investigation and resolution. The facilitator serves the participants and does not contribute information to the meeting.

Scribe/Modeler/Recorder/Documentation Expert: Records and publish the proceedings of the meeting and does not contribute information to the meeting.

Observers: Generally, members of the application development team assigned to the project. They are to sit behind the participants and are to silently observe the proceedings.

Key pre-workshop activities:[45]

1. **Identify the objectives of the workshop.** Set the scope and the business functions of the project. Assess both the project design and implementation complexity. Sizing of the project is important so that the design can be completed within 8 to 10 workshop days.

2. **Identify critical success factors.** Identify the critical success factors for both the technical aspect as well as the business aspect of the project. Determine how success will be measured.

3. **Define project deliverables.** The deliverables from the workshop are documentation and a design.

4. **Define the schedule of the workshop activities.** Workshops are generally from one to five days.

It usually takes at least three days for the participants to begin to be productive in their respective roles.

5. **Select the participants.** It is important to select participants that have enough knowledge and experience in the various business and technical areas so that they can make productive contributions to the project workshop.

6. **Prepare the workshop material.** The workshop material consists of documentation, worksheets, diagrams, and props to assists the participants in understanding the business function under investigation.

7. **Organize workshop activities and exercises.** Design workshop exercises and activities to provide initial deliverables that will build towards the final output of the workshop. It is up to the facilitator to mix and match the sub-team members to accomplish the organizational, cultural, and political objectives of the workshop. The facilitator must be able to build consensus and communications to bring issues out as early as possible in the process.

8. **Prepare, inform, and educate the workshop participants.** The participants will need to be briefed about the expected scope of the workshop at least 1 to 5 days before the workshop.

9. **Coordinate workshop logistics.** The workshop should be held off-site to avoid interruptions. The layout of the room must promote the communication and interaction required of the participants.

The advantages of the JAD methodology are attributed to the fast design technique and decrease in the costs associated with the requirements gathering process. One of the potential disadvantages is that the facilitator has to be able to motivate the participants and keep on a schedule that can be difficult feat.

__ITIL__

ITIL stands for **Information Technology Infrastructure Library** and describes procedures, tasks and checklists that are not organization-specific, used by an organization for establishing a minimum level of competency. It allows the organization to establish a baseline from which it can plan, implement, and measure. It is used to demonstrate compliance and to measure improvement.[46]

There are five volumes that compose the ITIL v3, published in May 2007 and updated in July 2011 for consistency:[47]

1. ITIL Service Strategy
2. ITIL Service Design
3. ITIL Service Transition
4. ITIL Service Operation
5. ITIL Continual Service Improvement

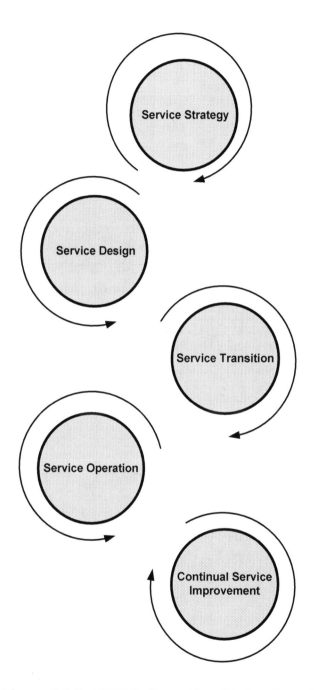

Figure 16-5. (ITIL) Information Technology Infrastructure Library v3 Model

Service Strategy

Service Strategy focuses on helping IT organizations improve and develop over the long term. Topics include service value definition, business-case development, service assets, market analysis, and service provider types.

Service Design

Service Design is understood to encompass all elements relevant to technology service delivery, rather than focusing solely on design of the technology itself. It addresses how a planned service solution interacts with the larger business and technical environments, service management systems required to support the service, processes that interacts with the service, technology, and architecture required to support the service, and the supply chain required to support the planned service.

Service Transition

Service Transition relates to the delivery of services required by a business into live/operational use, and often encompasses the "project" side of IT rather then "Business as usual". This area also covers topics such as managing changes to the "Business as usual" environment.

Service Operation

Service Operation provides best practice for achieving the delivery of agreed levels of services both to end-users and the customers (where "customers" refer to those individuals who pay for the service and negotiate the

SLA's). It is the part of the lifecycle where the services and value is actually directly delivered.

Continual Service Improvement (CSI)

Continual Service Improvement aims to align and realign IT services to changing business needs by identifying and implementing improvements to the IT "Submittal" services that support the business processes. The perspective on improvement is the business perspective of service quality, even though CSI aims to improve process effectiveness, efficiency and cost effectiveness of the IT processes through the whole lifecycle. CSI should clearly define what should be controlled and measured.

There are several criticism of ITIL. It has been noted that because of ITIL's primary focus on service management, ITIL has limited utility in managing poorly designed enterprise architectures, or how to feed back into the design of the enterprise architecture. ITIL does not directly address the business applications, which run on the IT infrastructure, nor does it facilitate a more collaborative working relationship between development and operations teams.

Next Act

There are far too many companies in operation that truly think that they have an operational methodology in use. But the truth is that most companies don't understand how the methodology is suppose to work. Ask the question;—What are the strengths and weaknesses of what they are using? Without knowing this how would you know if that is the best methodology for the program or project that you are working on? How would you know if the magic act that you are about to do is right for that particular audience? Remember, one size does not fit all projects in most organizations. Understand the culture, understand the methodologies, understand the organization's strategy and how to apply project management to drive the strategic goals and maybe, just maybe the customer's will come back for the next show.

References

1   Palladium Group, "Strategy Focused Organization Assessment", 2007, http://www.bscol.com.

2   Palladium Group, "How to Measure and Manage Human Capital for Strategic Advantage", 2007, http://www.bscol.com.

3   "ITL V3 Overview", August 7, 2007, itSMF, Available: http://www.itsmfi.org/files/itSMF_ITILV3_Intro_Overview.pdf.

4   Dave Mote, "New Organizational Models", http://www.referenceforbusiness.com.

5   Kenneth Knight, <u>Matrix Management: A Cross-functional Approach to Organization</u>. Great Britain:Gower, 1977.

6   Ibid.

7   Jeff Fields, *How Matrix Management Works*, online, CIO, Internet, 15 July 2002, Available: http://www.cio.com.

8   Jeffrey Pfeffer and Robert Sutton. *The Knowing-Doing Gap* (Harvard College UP, 2000) 18.

9   "The Real Meaning of On-the-Job Training," *Leader to Leader* (fall 1998): 61.

10 Thomas Davenport and Laurence Prusak. "Working Knowledge—How Organizations Manage What They Know," rev. of by Maviese Fisher. *Project Management Journal* 31.3 (Sept. 2000): 56.

11 Susan Bloch and Philip Whitely. *How to Manage in a Flat World* (FT Press, 2009) xxii.

12 ASTARO Internet Security. *The Dark Side of Cloud Computing,* Online. Internet. 2010. Available: http://

www.astaro.com/landingpages/en-worldwide-essential-firewall.

13   Wikipedia encyclopedia. *"Cloud computing"*, Issues / Privacy, Internet, 13 Sept. 2010, Available: http://en.wikipedia.org/wiki/Cloud_computing.

14   Leslie Cauley. *"NSA has massive database of Americans' phone calls"*, USAtoday.com, Internet, 10 May 2006. Available: http://www.usatoday.com/news/washington/2006-05-10-nsa.

15   Wikipedia encyclopedia.*"Cloud computing"*, Google and I.B.M. Join in 'Cloud Computing' Research, Internet, 8 Oct. 2007. Available: http://www.nytimes.com/.

16   Wikipedia encyclopedia. *"Cloud computing"*, <u>Cloud Computing Confusion Leads to Opportunity</u>, Network World—Gartner Report, Internet, 8 Jul. 2008. Available: http://www.networkworld.com/newsletters.

17   Wikipedia encyclopedia. *"Cloud computing"*, <u>Gartner Says Worldwide IT Spending On Pace to Surpass $3.4 Trillion in</u> 2008, Internet, Gartner, 18 Aug. 2008. Available: http://www.gartner.com.

18   Ocraworldwide. *"About Offshore Companies"*

19   Evan Campbell, The Top 3 Cost-Cutting Mistakes CIO's Make *And How to Avoid Them*, Internet, bitpipe, 21 Oct. 2010. Available: http//viewer.bitpipe.com.

20   MSN Money partner, *The labor market is slowly recovering, but with low-wage jobs. The US has lost at least 3 million high paid jobs forever.* 23 May 2011. Available: http//MSN.com.

21   Margo Visitacion and Tim DeGennaro, "The Forrester Wave™ Project Portfolio Management, Q4 2009.

22   Ibid.

23   RPM Systems Corporation, Employing *The Standard for Portfolio Management* to Expand Strategic Throughput, PMI Global Congress—North America 2009.

24   Adam Bookman, "Project Portfolio Management: Three Dangerous Myths",CIO (Feb. 2010), Available:http://www.cio.com.

25   Joe Thomas revised by Scott B. Droege, "Reference for Business". *Encyclopedia of Business* 2ⁿᵈ ed. (Mar. 2007). Available: http://www.cio.com.

26   Ibid.

27 Scott McEwen, "Requirements: An Introduction", *developerWorks*". (Apr 2004). Available: http://www. developerWorks.

28 Ibid.

29 Ibid.

30 Ibid.

31 Software Development Life Cycle (SDLC), Available:http:// docs.google.com/viewer?

32 Agile software development, Available:http//en.wikipedia. org/Agile_software_development

33 Ibid.

34 Ibid.

35 Systems development life-cycle,Available:http// en.wikipedia.org/Systems_development_life-cycle.

36 Ibid.

37 Ibid.

38 Waterfall model, Available:http//en.wikiedia.org/Waterfall_ model

39 Ibid.

40 Ibid.

41 Ibid.

42 Ibid.

43 Joint application design, Available:http//en.wikipedia.org/ Joint_application_design

44 Ibid.

45 Ibid.

46 Ibid.

47 Ibid.

INDEX

About the Author

Maviese Fisher is an Independent Program Manager with extensive experience in strategic resource and budget planning, project risk and cost analysis, team moral, personnel management, progress assessments and workflow analysis. She has managed national and international engagements with responsibilities in creating and delivering on implementation programs and processes across the United States in the Financial, Health, Pharmaceutical, Legal, Manufacturing, Distribution, Automotive, Advertising, Education and Government industries. She has worked as an Systems Engineer for IBM managing technology implementation projects receiving several quality and service awards, Director for local government, Senior Program Manager for HP managing international programs and as a Board member on the Business as an Agent of World Benefit (B.A.W.B) at Case Western Reserve University. Maviese holds an International MBA and a BA in Tele-Communications from Baldwin Wallace College and a BS in Physics. She is a certified Project Manager and has served on the Project Management Institute Board Nominating Committee. She is published as a contributor in the 2006 edition of "The Standard for Program Management, PMI Global Standard", creating the international standards for Programs and Portfolios. She has developed and taught project management, educational, application and technical training courses for several industries.